DIG DEEP, BUILD HIGH

FROM THE BEGINNING

ALISA J. HENLEY

© 2016 by Alisa Henley All rights reserved

Printed in the United States ALL RIGHTS RESERVED

No part of this publication may be reproduced, stored in a retrieval system, or transmitted, in any form or by any means—electronic, mechanical, photocopying, recording, or otherwise—without written permission.

ISBN 978-1-5369-9531-2
For information:
Alisa J. Henley
PO Box 683, Grandview, MO 64030

Mail to: info@alisahenley.com

TABLE OF CONTENTS

Chapter 1	From the Beginning	9
Chapter 2	Side Hustle to Main Hustle	25
Chapter 3	Top 10 Truths	35
Chapter 4	Nonprofit Leaders	45
Chapter 5	Don't Choose Failure	59
Chapter 6	Plan to Succeed	69
Chapter 7	Business Branding	81

Information for this book was drawn from a number sources:

- Small Business Administration

- Fidelity Charitable

- Project Smart

- Marketing Bootcamp

INTRODUCTION

Dig Deep, Build High (From the Beginning) was inspired by many conversations held with a variety of small business owners and leaders of organizations. Many people start businesses and organizations without a clear understanding of how to ensure that they are sustainable and that the foundations on which they are established will not crack at some point. While contemplating writing this book, I was reminded of the fairy tale "The Three Little Pigs." All three pigs built a house, but they all used different types of materials. When the wolf came to terrorize them, he was successful in blowing down the two houses made of straw and sticks, but he was not able to destroy the third pig's house, which was made of brick.

Think of your organization or business like the houses the three little pigs built. They all had a vision for a house and each one of them selected their desired material to build with. However, only one of the houses had strong enough material to withstand the pressure of the wolf blowing on it. When starting a business or organization, you have to think like the third little pig and anticipate what will happen when pressure arises. Will your establishment easily be blown away, or will it stand the test of time? I am sure the third little pig was thinking like a builder and mapping out the best way to protect his investment.

A builder either designs or purchases architectural plans to build a structure. The builder's blueprint for success is the written plan that they are following. However, before the building process starts, he or she must first determine the width and depth of the foundation to be poured. The taller the building, the deeper and thicker the foundation must be. When erecting businesses and organizations, we use the same process with different language. Creating the initial blueprint for your establishment is imperative because you will need to have a map of what it looks like. Going back in time to when I started my first business, I did not go into it with a blueprint. In fact, I immediately started working in my business without giving any consideration to having a plan. Needless to say, five years down the line, I was forced to embark upon a process that I should have completed within the first year of starting. At this point, the process was much more intense and time-consuming. Dismantling what was already built and rebuilding it is a very daunting task.

Most entrepreneurs miss the mark by not laying the proper foundation from the beginning. Like me, we register with the state, get our EIN, and start doing business, only focusing on the short-term. Immediately, the goal is to make money for your business or acquire funding if you start a nonprofit. Every business owner and organization founder should create a business model, envision growth, and know the long-term impact of their venture. When God gave me the vision to start a business, I didn't know where to start, but someone came along who had my answer. For that, I am eternally grateful. There were some things that I knew, but I lacked the experience and wisdom to execute them. I knew I needed to track my income, but I had no knowledge about QuickBooks. My knowledge and experience was very limited because every place I worked had already been established upon the foundation it was designed for. I now had to pour and build upon my own foundation. Over the years, I have come to discover that there are some basic foundational necessities that we all must implement when starting our organizations, regardless of the size or if they are faith-based or community-based.

Dig Deep, Build High *(From the Beginning)* is a book that is written to guide each person through the process of establishing a firm foundation for their business and/or organization. In this book, you will learn about registering your business with the state and getting your EIN if you haven't already done so, you will learn the difference between a business plan and a strategic plan and if you need one or both, and you will learn the basic foundational elements of setting goals and accomplishing those goals so that your business can grow. This book will become an invaluable tool that you carry around with you or keep close by, knowing that when you run into a challenging obstacle, you have it there to guide you through the process of overcoming that challenge.

Are you ready to become a builder?

CHAPTER ONE
FROM THE BEGINNING

Starting a business is an incredibly exciting opportunity that brings its own set of risks and challenges. The undertaking can be massive and life-changing, to say the least. However, being your own boss, controlling your time, and creating earning potential doing what you love are some of the advantages that can make the venture completely worthwhile. It is not without planning, creativity, and hard work that you will achieve great success. Successful business owners have certain skills in common. Most are comfortable with taking risks as beginners. You would be responsible for making all of the major decisions, realizing that there is a high level of uncertainty regarding the outcomes. If you are afraid to take risks and deal with the shady areas of life, then entrepreneurship may not be a good fit for you. Being able to accept rejection is a key characteristic as well. There is also a necessity for embracing independence. One of my surreal moments was when I realized that I had to now cover the expenses of attending conferences, enrolling in training programs, and maintaining my own certifications.

The ability to persuade and negotiate is an entrepreneur's saving grace. Having the greatest idea in the world is wonderful if you can convince others to support it. You will have to negotiate everything, and I do mean everything. Polished negotiation skills will help you save money and keep your business running smoothly. Public speaking, engaging new people with ease, and presenting compelling information is paramount to making your idea a success. Starting out, I had no clue about how to negotiate. I really did not learn until I became a part-time real estate agent. Before, I just walked away and never tried to reach middle ground until I learned that keeping the deal alive is always the ultimate goal.

Lastly, having a strong support system before stepping out has been proven to strengthen one's position as an entrepreneur. Within the first couple of months of branching out, you will be faced with many decisions and simply need to bounce ideas off someone. When I started out, I found multiple sources of assistance to help me through these beginning stages. I had a business mentor, a local support system made up of family and friends, and a network of other small business owners I met through a program offered by the Chamber of Commerce.

> *Having the **greatest** idea in the world is **wonderful** if you can convince others to support it.*

Do you think you are ready to become an entrepreneur and start your own business? If so, ask yourself these 20 questions developed by the Small Business Administration (SBA):

1. Why am I starting a business?

2. What kind of business do I want?

3. Who is my ideal customer?

4. What products or services will my business provide?

5. Am I prepared to spend the time and money needed to get my business started?

6. What differentiates my business idea and the products or services I will provide from others?

7. Where will my business be located?

8. How many employees will I need?

9. What types of suppliers do I need?

10. How much money do I need to get started?

11. Will I need to get a loan?

12. How soon will it be before my products or services are available?

13. How long do I have until I start making a profit?

14. Who is my competition?

15. How will I price my product compared to my competition?

16. How will I set up the legal structure of my business?

17. What taxes do I need to pay?

18. What kind of insurance do I need?

19. How will I manage my business?

20. How will I advertise my business?

If you are ready to move forward, the next thing you must understand is that there are basically two types of organizations: for-profit (business) and nonprofit (charitable).

For-Profit (Business) Organizations

A for-profit organization exists to make money and build wealth, meaning the business is designed for revenue to greatly exceed expenses. Owners of for-profit businesses decide how the additional moneys are disbursed. For example, they can take the money for themselves, invest it back into the business, or create some type of incentive plan for the employees. For-profit businesses can be structured in six different ways.

Sole Proprietorship: A sole proprietorship is the most basic type of business to establish. You alone own the company and are responsible for its assets and liabilities.

Cooperative: A cooperative is formed to meet a collective need or to provide a service that benefits all member-owners.
Corporation: A corporation (known as a C corporation under tax law) is more complex and generally suggested for larger, established companies with multiple employees.

Partnership: There are several different types of partnerships, which depend on the nature of the arrangement and partner responsibility for the business.

S Corporation: An S Corporation is similar to a C corporation, but you are taxed only on the personal level.

The business structure you choose will have legal and tax implications.

Nonprofit (Charitable) Organizations

A nonprofit organization exists for charitable reasons and is community-based. In a nonprofit, moneys received cannot be distributed to owners. After meeting overhead expenses, the majority of revenue must be invested back into the organization to help perform their mission. The only nonprofits that are automatically considered tax-exempt are churches. Individuals who donate to churches can automatically use what they give as a tax deduction. All other nonprofits must complete the tax-exemption—501(c) (3) application with the IRS before those who give can have a tax deduction. As the organizer of a nonprofit, you decide if you want to pursue tax exemption status after registering with your state. Tax-exempt nonprofit corporations can (and do) operate in all other particulars like any other sort of business. They have bank accounts, own productive assets of all kinds, receive income from sales and other forms of activity (including donations and grants if they are successful at finding that sort of support), make and hold passive investments, employ staff, and enter into contracts.

...even with the plethora of risks and uncertainties that come with it, being an entrepreneur is still very attractive to the average person...

The next three steps you will engage in is choosing a business name, registering with your state, and acquiring your EIN. Choosing a business name is so important in this process because the name is what will start the branding process for you. Therefore, you should give it careful consideration. Businesses do change their names after the fact, but keep in mind that every time you make changes to your name and/or mission, the branding process starts over in some aspects. Your customers must acquaint themselves with the new identity. You should also give a thought to whether it's web-ready. Is the domain name even available? Yes, I am suggesting that you research domains before finalizing your business name. You will need to claim your social media web identity as early as possible.

Because many businesses start as side hustles, solo operations, or freelancers, you can also default to using your personal name, and many do. However, using your personal name makes it difficult to build a professional brand and create awareness. Consider the following:

How will your name look? On the web, as part of a logo, on social media.

What connotations does it evoke? Is your name too corporate or not corporate enough? Does it reflect your business philosophy and culture? Does it appeal to your market?

Is it unique? Pick a name that hasn't been claimed by others, online or offline. A quick web search and domain name search (more on this below) will alert you to any existing use.

Your next step in the process is to register your entity with the state you live in. Some cities require registration as well. I can't tell you how many people say that they have a business but have never officially registered it with the state. They are selling products and services, but there is nothing official regarding their legal right to conduct business in the state. You are required to register your for-profit or nonprofit with the Secretary of State. Most states give you the option of doing this online. You will need to put a physical address on the form; PO boxes are not accepted.

The last step before you can start doing business is to secure your Employer Identification Number (EIN). Some new business owners do this first, but I recommend that you do it last. The name on your EIN must match what you registered with the state. What if your name is not available with the state and you already have your EIN? Just a thought. You can obtain your EIN directly from the IRS website. For-profits and nonprofits alike can start doing business once they are registered with the state and have acquired their EIN. By doing it online, you can complete your registrations and start doing business all in the same day. However, to open a bank account, for-profits may need an operating agreement (depending on the bank), and nonprofits will need to present bylaws.

Note: There is an additional step for nonprofits. A 501(c) (3) application must be submitted if you desire tax exemption status. Also, depending on your business, there could be federal and/or state licenses that you have to apply for.

The final foundational matter that we will discuss in this chapter is creating a business plan. According to research, approximately 80% of business owners get started without one. Business plans are required by banking institutions if business owners are securing upfront capital, but for those who start solo and are not seeking funding, they are usually not a priority. However, whether you are seeking funding or not, it is important to have a business plan. It will be your roadmap of how you intend to grow your revenue and market your organization. If you are requesting a loan, you will need to complete your plan right away. If not, you should develop your plan within the first year of operation. You can find many templates on the internet, but whichever you choose, make sure that your plan contains the following standard sections:

Executive Summary: Your executive summary is a snapshot of your business plan as a whole and touches on your company profile and goals. Read these tips about what to include.

Company Description: Your company description provides information on what you do, what differentiates your business from others, and the markets your business serves.

Market Analysis: Before launching your business, it is essential for you to research your business industry, market, and competitors.

Organization & Management: Every business is structured differently. Find out the best organizational and management structure for your business.

Service or Product Line: What do you sell? How does it benefit your customers? What is the product lifecycle? Get tips on how to tell the story about your product or service.

Marketing & Sales: How do you plan to market your business? What is your sales strategy? Read more about how to include this information in your plan.

Funding Request: If you are seeking funding for your business, find out about the necessary information you should include in your plan.

Financial Projections: If you need funding, providing financial projections to back up your request is critical. Find out what information you need to include in your financial projections for your small business.

Appendix: An appendix is optional, but it is a useful place to include information such as resumes, permits and leases. Find additional information you should include in your appendix.

I recall hearing millions of reasons why I should not go into business for myself. People told me I would acquire debt, have trouble paying my health insurance, possibly lose everything if I didn't succeed . . . the list goes on. However, even with the plethora of risks and uncertainties that come with it, being an entrepreneur is still very attractive to the average person. Initially, your work hours will be longer and your pay will be less, but if you stick to the grind, it will all gradually balance out. You will learn how to command your day and time. Running your own business allows you to tell your story. Everyone will want to know what you do and how you got started. The best part is that you decide how to tell the story. There is nothing more rewarding than painting your own picture. Taking advantage of tax benefits is another piece of the puzzle that makes being a business owner attractive. Building something successfully from the ground up produces the greatest sense of pride one could have, and it is something you can pass on to the next generation. Be proud of it. You created it.

Ready to Move Forward? Questions to Ask Yourself

☐ Am I a self-starter? Do I have the discipline to maintain a schedule?

☐ Do I want to earn more money? Will this business earn more money from the beginning or do I need to be prepared to initially work for less?

☐ Do I want to be more creative? Do I have the necessary skills to be successful in this business?

☐ Am I looking for more flexibility in my work and family schedule? Will this business allow me to work the schedule I desire?

☐ Am I ready for different challenges and adventures? Am I prepared to respond quickly to the needs of my business?

☐ Have I discussed this proposed business with my family?

☐ Do I have the money needed for business startup and initial operating expenses until I start earning a profit?

Startup Phase

☐ Registration: Decide upon the legal structure of your business. Choose a business name and register your business with the appropriate state and/or federal agencies.

☐ Property: If your business will be selling, renting or leasing tangible personal property, you must obtain the proper state sales tax license from the Department of Revenue and determine if a separate local sales tax license is required. A sales tax license is also required if you rent accommodations for less than 30 days.

☐ Taxes: Be aware of the personal and business tax implications of starting your own business. Self-employment tax will double an individual's contribution to social security and Medicare taxes. Property tax is collected on all personal property owned by a business.

☐ Licenses: Find out if there are any special licenses required for the business you are starting.

☐ Location: Determine the best location for your business. You can get information about traffic patterns on state highways. Some local governments have information on city and county roads. They may also have information on local population demographics. Observe pedestrian movement during business hours to estimate walk-in potential.

☐ Regulations: Check with the local city and county government regarding any special business regulations, sales taxes, personal property taxes, and zoning restrictions affecting your business.

☐ Management: Seek management advice and counseling.

Assembling Your Team of Professional Advisors

☐ Find an accountant.

☐ Find a lawyer.

☐ Find an insurance broker.

☐ Find a real estate agent.

☐ Develop a financial plan and include profit and loss projections, cash flow analysis, and capital requirements. What type of financing will your business need? What financing options are realistic for your situation?

☐ Identify your liability risks. Obtain adequate insurance coverage. Protect your business activities far enough in advance to cover your growth.

☐ Protect your intellectual property rights through proper registration and maintenance. These pertain to your ideas, products, symbols, and logos.

☐ Prepare a business plan.

☐ Write your business plan.

☐ Determine who will buy the product or service you are offering.

☐   Define the strengths and weaknesses of your business.

☐   Consider these questions: Why is this a good business idea? What is the opportunity in the marketplace? Why is the opportunity present now?

☐   Consider further: What difficulties could potentially arise? What might cause them? How will you deal with them? What will be their effect on the business?

☐   Create a three-year budget and cash flow forecast (often very difficult at the outset, but banks like to see a medium term plan).

☐   Establish a capital requirement and funding proposal that answers these questions: How much? Where from? How long? What cost? How will you repay?

☐   Consider shareholders: Who will be shareholders? Are the minority shareholders happy with proposals? Have you a proper shareholders' agreement to record exactly what you have agreed?

☐   Consider directors: Who will be directors? Are directors aware of their responsibilities as directors? If not employees, what will they be paid? What will you be paid?

☐   Consider staff: What other staff will be needed? At first? Later?

☐   Consider space: What space will be needed? What will it cost? What other terms?

☐ Prepare a marketing plan.

☐ Establish a three-year plan to support the business plan.

☐ Analyze sales by customers/sources of sales.

☐ Analyze sales by product or service.

☐ Remember extra staff when needed.

☐ Look realistically at marketing costs—do your homework and be accurate.

Journal Entry

What did you learn in this chapter?

How will you use this information?

What are your goals after reading this chapter?

1.

2.

3.

CHAPTER TWO
SIDE HUSTLE TO MAIN HUSTLE

A large number of successful business owners start their business while still working their day job because the day job pays the bills and gives your loved ones bragging rights at different functions. Most of our businesses started from a side hustle. A side hustle is a way to make some extra money that allows you the flexibility to pursue what you're most interested in. It can give you a chance to explore your true passion without quitting your day job. Most side hustles start from a passion, project, or idea that makes you light up inside and soaks up more and more of your creative energy. I started my side hustle being a contract trainer while still working a full-time job. I accepted a contract to facilitate leadership development training for two years before deciding to leave my job and become an independent contractor.

A person may start a cleaning business, real estate company, or catering business on the side for fun. However, juggling work and a side hustle is challenging to say the least. Navigating that road can make you feel like you're biking up the tallest, steepest mountain you can find. Therefore, you cannot do it forever. Although there are some challenges to having a full-time job and a side hustle, there are some hidden benefits as well. One of the main draws to starting is the option of bringing extra income into your household. Another reason is to exercise your plan "B" as it relates to your career. A side hustle might be the perfect opportunity to shield yourself against unemployment. As you can imagine, job security is not what it used to be. In years past, you could maintain a job for 20 or 30 years and have your choice of retirement. Today, the average length that a person will stay on the job is three to five years. In some cases, they voluntarily leave, and in others, they are terminated.

People pour their heart and soul into a career without having a plan "B." When their job, for whatever reason, is taken away, they find themselves back in the job market. Being back in the job market sometimes mean going back to school to acquire additional skills, knowledge, and abilities. This proves why side hustles are great opportunities. You can increase the amount of time that you invest in your hustle to earn additional income that keeps you afloat until you can figure out your next move. Side hustles help to build confidence and develop marketable skills for you to fall back on. They also create new passions that move you from hobby level to income insurance.

The last benefit that I will discuss is that side hustles help you to develop professionally. Prior to becoming a contract trainer, I never facilitated any type of training. In fact, the only presentations I participated in was in college with other students. I remember it like it was yesterday, being asked to develop and facilitate leadership training. I asked, "Do you think I can do it?" The answer was "Yes! You have the perfect personality to be a trainer." I accepted the contract and was unleashed to over 200 participants my first time out of the gate. To my surprise, the evaluations were glowing. This one assignment spanned over two years. Fourteen years down the line, I get calls from all across the United States to either facilitate training, deliver keynotes, or host workshops. The rest is history. My two-year side hustle became my main hustle. Even if you have no expectation of your side hustle replacing your primary job, it will change the course of your career. Your side hustle can add value to your day job and give you an opportunity to practice continued professional development.

I encourage others to seek a side hustle to add variety to their work life. It is instrumental in offering a creative outlet to allow for professional and personal development. The benefits will go far beyond what you could ever imagine, not to mention the immediate cash boost you can get from taking on extra work. If you are thinking about a side hustle, consider and answer these three questions:

- ✓ What do I want to do?

- ✓ How much time can I invest?

- ✓ How much money do I need to bring in?

Coming up with the type of side hustle you desire is the least of your worries. It is more important for you to determine what your strengths are and the best way that you can use them in your side hustle. For example, if you have a talent to create flyers and you do it as a hobby, you may consider making that your side hustle and marketing that skill to other small businesses or authors. Keep in mind that you should not allow your side hustle to overextend you to the point that you are giving more time to it than you dedicate to your full-time job or the running of your household. The most important decision you will have to make is how much you are you willing to invest and what you are willing to sacrifice for your side hustle.

Even if you have no expectation of your side hustle replacing your primary job, it will change the course of your career.

Your answers will depend on why you started the side hustle. Did you start it to pay off debt? To make ends meet? Or, did you start it to eventually take the place of your full-time job? Once you have evaluated why you started the side hustle, you will be closer to deciding how much money you desire to make. If you started the side hustle to eventually take the place of your full-time job, then you will need to determine how much money you need to make over a period of time.

There are three signs to be aware of when contemplating your side hustle becoming your main hustle. Jessica Knoll, author of *Luckiest Girl Alive*, shared in an interview the three signals that gave her clarity on when it was time for her to switch gears from a full-time job into uncharted territory, turning her side hustle into her main hustle. The first thing she shared is that it may be time to transition when you are essentially working two full-time jobs, but your side hustle is providing steady income, as well as keeping you busy and motivated.

The second sign is when the return on your side hustle is or could potentially be larger than the return on your full-time job. In her case, she worked a full-time job while authoring a book that became very successful, eventually leading to a movie contract. She took time to digest becoming a novelist before leaving her employer. She enjoyed going to work, but in reality, releasing the book opened another door. Because the opportunity presented was very lucrative, Jessica concluded it was time to make the transition.

The last sign that Jessica Knoll shared is when you're financially prepared to quit your full-time job and you're willing to do it gracefully. When you leave your job, always leave in a way where you can return if need be. I recommend at least giving a thirty-day notice so that you have time to leave things in order, making sure that your successor will not be overwhelmed. When

I branched out, I stayed until I hired my successor and offered to work on a part-time basis to ensure my replacement's success. I was heartbroken to leave my full-time job because these people had become like family to me, but I knew that if I stayed, I would potentially regret it. I didn't know what the future held or how my career would evolve with that particular employer, but I am glad I took the risk. I followed the signs that it was time for me to make my side hustle my main hustle.

Turning your side hustle into your main hustle is a scary thought, and in most cases, you have to be prepared to either sink or swim. Your main hustle is how you cover your expenses and provide for your family. Making the decision to pursue my side hustle was easy for me because I was financially prepared. However, your situation might be different, leaving you to weigh out another set of circumstances. It is normal that the hobby artist who decides to go into business painting murals, the novice baker who decides to make cakes on the side, and you, whatever your unique situation may be, would struggle with making this decision. Even if you have planned, the fight in your mind is still fierce. When you transition from side hustle to main hustle, that river of income must be solid, profitable, sustainable, and professional.

If you're currently straddling the line between being an employee and being a boss man or lady, I can't tell you what to do, but if pursuing your side hustle is something you frequently think about, it's probably time to at least try and make it happen. Here are a few things I learned through my own experience that will help you make the leap.

Become a part-time pro. Getting to the place where you have to sacrifice time in another area in order to make more money is a great thing. Consider taking the leap of faith. On the other hand, if your side hustle is still in the infancy stages without a consistent flow of income, then continue to work.

Work the numbers. In addition to paying yourself a salary, think about the cost of covering your benefits and paying self-employment taxes.

Save. It's traditional entrepreneurial wisdom to save money before you start your business, but I think it's just as important to save once you're out on your own. When you start a business of any kind, there will be ups and downs. Personally, I have plentiful months and some lean months. Also, some clients will not pay on time, and you will have to absorb the wait.

Find resources. Finding free resources is difficult, but they do exist. Seek resources for help drafting contracts, doing graphic design work, accounting, business strategy development, and/or legal services. Look for local and online resources. We try to do it all, but the reality is that we can't.

Don't take things personally. Or try not to, at least, and don't be your own worst critic. Your support may not come from the direction you expect. I struggled when those close to me were not coming to my rescue. Another area I had to balance was taking negative feedback personally. When you work for yourself, you are your work. Therefore, when you lose a client or admit you have room for improvement, it hits the heart. If your emotions are all over the board, then maybe entrepreneurship is not for you.

Invest in your business. Don't fret about having to spend money on things that make your life easier when you're starting out. It will make you feel like you are eating into the profit and spending money you need to save. However, if something will truly make your business more organized, help you multitask, and spread the word about your services, if you can afford it without skipping a rent payment, then do it.

Set up an office space. It is absolutely necessary for you to have a dedicated place to work. Twelve years down the road, I still get up every morning, get dressed, and go to my office in the basement of my home. I have work hours and a place to focus with minimal distractions.

Find good help. You may need to find others to help float you and your business at times. At some point, the work may overwhelm you or life will happen. When I broke my ankle, I had to hire a contractor to assume some of my work. Even today, I still hire contractors to perform various services for me.

Enjoy it. Adapting quickly to changes that happen in your life and business is monumental. Some days, I take my laptop to the lake. Love and enjoy the flexibility you have. You can choose the people you work with, when you work, and where you work. And I really try to enjoy it all.

Journal Entry

Do you have a side hustle? If no, are you thinking about starting one? Why?

How can you use the information in this chapter?

What are your goals after reading this chapter?

1.

2.

3.

CHAPTER THREE
TOP 10 TRUTHS

I've had several conversations with business owners and leaders of community and faith-based nonprofits. I asked them all what they would do differently if they started over. This led to a reflection of what a top 10 list regarding starting a business or organization would look like. Therefore, I deemed it important to include such a list in this book. Five years after starting my first business, I came across a list published by Lynn Vos discussing 10 things that all small business owners should know. After reading this article, I was empowered, received the instruction, comprehended the knowledge, and applied the wisdom. I cannot take credit for this list, but I am adding my own perspective regarding the meaning and application of what Vos suggested.

Regardless of the type of company or organization you are starting, there are some basic truths every entrepreneurial spirit should know. Organizers and leaders of businesses and nonprofits alike must know that they are accountable for the integrity of what they are building.

1.

No one will look after your money the way you will. You should seek advice about revenue building strategies, but ultimately you are responsible for ensuring that you are a good steward of any income or investment associated with your business or organization. For example, you have to maintain fair business practices and be reasonable with customers when pricing your products and services. If you have started or are starting a for-profit business, the IRS will hold you responsible for what your accountant was hired to do. Leaders of nonprofits with a 501(c)(3) are responsible for making sure regulations for donors are followed. Remember that it is your responsibility to oversee the work for which you hired or contracted others to complete on behalf of the business or organization.

Think about the famous people who have passed away in recent years that you thought died wealthy. Like me, you were probably shocked to hear the news reports that they were poor at the time of death. These legends gave others stewardship over their wealth, leaving them poor and robbing them of the ability to leave a legacy for their families. They made money but did not dedicate the time to watch over their finances. Overseeing the financial aspects of your investment is key to your success. You should always know what is going on within the financial structure of your business or organization.

2.

There is always competition. Businesses, organizations, and nonprofits will always have competition. It doesn't matter what you offer or say or who is in your customer base. Other entities will offer the same or similar products or services that you offer. In some cases, they may be able to beat your prices or fees. Don't ever think that you have a monopoly, because you do not. Your goal is to determine how to change the game in your

Organizers and *leaders* of businesses and nonprofits alike must know that they are **accountable** for the **integrity** of what they are building.

favor. What can you do to make your product or service more attractive to customers?

3.

If you are not moving and improving, you are losing ground. The world around you is continuously in motion. People are constantly moving and shaking. Every day, you should be thinking of ways to improve your products and services and seeking growth strategies. Every morning, you should wake up and work on your business. It doesn't matter if you are in the planning or operational stage. When I first started, I did not have any clients, but I worked daily on developing leadership training programs, even though I had no one to deliver them to. Now, twelve years down the line, I am using everything I developed. I knew that one day, the clients would come, so I had to be proactive. Taking action early saves you time and money in the long run. When your clients arrive, you are ready. You have what they need, now it is a matter of customizing it.

I committed the words "persistent" and "consistent" to my heart and work during this stage of establishing a firm foundation for my business. You have to constantly move if you want to gain ground and be a successful business owner. You always have to be working toward your vision.

4.

All new technology is not necessarily good technology for you. Today, technology is tremendous, and personally, I can hardly keep up with it. You don't have to either. I received the best advice about this from a young man who started a company to help small businesses with technology and social media. Are you ready for it? He said to abstain from plugging into every social media site and to stick with the ones you understand and are good at. At the time, I had accounts with every social media site out there, but I only used Facebook, LinkedIn, and Twitter. I also had software programs that I had no idea how to use because I was trying to save money. I quickly realized that the time invested in trying to learn them took away from me working on my vision. It was less expensive for me to pay someone to do it for me.

Concentrating on aspects of technology that will help you to become more efficient and build your customer base should be your priority. Making this shift will help you focus on process and results rather than trying to keep up with technology. As small business owners, we always say we have more time than money and we get in the habit of trying to do everything. However, if technology is not our area of expertise, it's going to be difficult for us to do all of those things.

5.

What matters is what the customer wants, not what you want. We are all in the people business. People will enter and exit, all wanting the same thing: customer satisfaction. Don't forget the customer votes in your wallet. Without customers, you will not have any staying power, let alone building power.

6.

The time to seek legal or professional advice is before you sign on the dotted line. Over and over again, I've seen business owners sign contracts without a clear understanding of the impact of what they are signing. The best advice I can give to you is this: Don't be so in love with the idea, business, property, or circumstances that you don't exercise wisdom. Not everyone will take time to explain documents to you. If they do, there is still no guarantee that what they are saying will match up with what is written. Do not sign based on explanation alone; review the document, and if there is doubt, ask for a couple of days to review and consider. Once you sign contracts, it's hard to get out of them, and you become liable for whatever you put your signature on.

7.

Being in business or having an organization is pointless unless it is bringing in revenue or funding. You cannot forget the basics of making your cash register ring or receiving checks from your clients. It is very easy to get distracted by administrative things. For example, you can get tied up with making things pretty and forget about networking to bring in new clients or customers. The bottom line is that you are in business to make money, so if you are in business and you're not making money, you need to refigure your strategy. Without sales, income, and revenue, there can be no business.

8.

Image minus performance equals dissolution. Dressing up your logo and website and building a brand is great and necessary. However, success must be measured and not just seen. Your personal image matters as well. We like to put our nice clothes on, carry our nice briefcases, announce that we are business owners, pass out business cards, and tell others about our business. However, we must also have the ability to pass the benefits of our services or products to consumers. All things can be great in our business or organization, but if we are not performing, we are wasting our time and the time of others. Wasting time is just like wasting money.

9.

Conduct as many banking transactions as you can in person. Get to know people at your banking institution before you need them. Having a relationship with your banker before things get tough will open a door for them to go to bat for you because they know your strengths. Don't get me wrong, banking online is a good option, but having a person that is familiar with your banking trends is even better. Do not fall into the habit of doing everything in front of a screen. In business, face-to-face interaction is still proven to be the most effective. This advice was given to me many years down the road when I was in crisis.

10.

Whether you are on the winning or losing side, have a plan outlining how you will exit the business. On the winning side, a business may be flourishing, but the owner wants to go in a different direction. Yes, sometimes we outgrow our business or our interests change. We may opt to open up the business for purchase. On the losing side, a business may dissolve because it has not turned a profit for three years or more. In some cases, businesses cannot even break even. If your business is failing, you need to have an idea of how much you are willing to lose before pulling the plug.

If your business is winning, have an idea of its worth. This includes the value of your customer base and inventory. Have a figure in your head and on paper in case someone is interested in acquiring your business. It is like wanting to be debt-free. What if someone walked up to you and offered to pay all of your debt if you could give them the amount? Can you? Personally, I can get within a couple hundred dollars of the amount it would take for me to be totally debt-free. You should have this same mentality when it comes to the value of your business or organization. I know many people who have sold items that were valued at more than what they settled for.

I have often seen people sell businesses, only to find out later that they were worth more than what they sold for. You need to know what your value is.

Journal Entry

What was the most interesting concept in this chapter?

How will you apply the top 10 truths?

What are your goals after reading this chapter?

1.

2.

3.

CHAPTER FOUR
NONPROFIT LEADERS

Per the National Center of Charitable Statistics, there are more than 1.5 million nonprofit organizations in the world. If you look into established nonprofits, you will find more than one fighting your same cause and with a similar mission. Defining organizational goals will help steer your nonprofit in the right direction. Running a nonprofit means giving up control of your organization. The 10 things listed in this chapter are going to be monumental in helping you create, grow, or strengthen your nonprofit organization.

1.

Whether you are thinking about starting an organization, already have one, or are leading one, you should know that your nonprofit is a living organism. Your organization is mobile, just like your body parts. It has hands, feet, and vision. It breathes, sees, and smells. Not continually talking about the vision at hand gives the impression that the mission work of the nonprofit is dead. Talking about the nonprofit and its work keeps it living within the community. It gives it life and light. It is imperative that every person connected to the organization gives life to it because every living thing grows from the inside out. Mission work is a heart issue, with hands extended into the community.

2.

An organization will grow only to the size of its leader. Every leader of a nonprofit must strive to develop himself/herself in the area of leadership to broaden their horizons. Ask yourself, which areas can you stand to grow in? If leaders make it their mission to develop, the organization will have no choice but to grow. In turn, everyone connected to the organization will also grow and the mission work will expand.

3.

A leader creates value for the organization and others. That means that you're not only responsible for your growth and development, but you are also responsible for the growth and development of those who are around you. Helping others grow does not mean that you have to take on the task yourself. You can implement systems and programs that will assist in the development of others. It is not about you personally. It is about the impact your nonprofit has in the community and on associated people. You have to create value before you can expect others to value the mission work of your organization. Think of it as the initial investment you will make.

4.

Leaders of nonprofits and everyone supporting the mission are change leaders, not change agents. Change agents are driven by their need, while a change leader is driven by the value that change will bring. Change agents tend to make decisions out of being desperate or out of crisis. When you begin to make decisions based on being desperate or out of your need, then it becomes the house that the individual built and not the house that the organization or the community built. Therefore, you want to switch from being needs-driven to being value-driven. Every consideration should be centered on the value that it will bring to the organization, community, and stakeholder.

5.

Grant providers are not ATMs. There was a time when you could apply for a grant and automatically receive it. Funders would even fund your operating expenses. Today, however, they are only interested in supporting particular causes. One of the greatest misconceptions in the nonprofit world is that people think getting grants is easy and that they are given for anything. Believe it or not, many for-profits think there is grant money for them to start up. Do not fall into the trap of pursuing a grant for every need within the organization. The reality is that approximately 30% of the budget should come from grants. Just like you diversify your personal investments, you have to diversify the organization's revenue streams.

6.

Donors are not walking wallets. People no longer practice charitable giving as much as social investing. We all know people who have money, but they are going to direct it toward their passion. People invest in causes or organizations that help them to further their mission. For example, I started The Sunshine Organization. We engage in leadership development and capacity building for faith-based organizations. Donors who focus on saving animals are not going to donate to us because we do not save animals. We create, grow, and strengthen leaders. If you have a nonprofit that is only getting financial contributions from 20% of the members, then it is safe to assume that the other 80% is not committed to mission work. Many of them are probably giving to other organizations that further social causes they are more passionate about. It is important for organizations seeking funding to make sure they are practicing integrity. For example, if you are raising money to build a bookstore, make sure that it is built. If you're raising money to rehab a community, the money should not be used for something else. Donors lose faith in the integrity of the mission when they can't see the fruit of their giving. There are organizations who collect money for one reason but use it for another because they are driven by their needs.

7.

You cannot expect others to invest in your nonprofit if your leadership does not invest. For starters, your board of directors should financially invest. If you encounter a donor or an investor and ask them for money, one of the first questions they will ask is what you are investing personally or what your board is investing. If you own a house, you cannot ask someone to remodel your bathroom at their expense. If you are not willing to invest in your dwelling, how can you ask someone else to do so? Investing and funding occurs from the inside out.

8.

Program evaluation reveals outcomes and impact analysis unveils impact. Many times, nonprofits have programs, but the outcomes are not realized because impact is not measured. Measuring the impact lends itself to sustaining the program or operation. In addition, it gives you an opportunity to make changes to be more effective and increase your reach. Outcomes must be achieved and impact measured because they both demonstrate a return on the investment. Unfortunately, in smaller organizations, we overlook evaluating the investment. Funders and donors want proof of the benefit of what you are offering.

9.

There is no money in being the best kept secret. How many people know about the service you provide? How many people know about your organization? How many people know about your vision and your calls? Are you a secret? If people you run into say that they have not heard of you, that is a problem. Before you can increase your support, you must know if people are aware of your organization and what they think about it. Do not be afraid to seek feedback about your organization and the services you provide.

10.

Value is the difference between sustainability and extinction. Ask yourself if you want what you started to live beyond you. Do you want the organization to be sustained or become extinct? Everything you do and every decision you make in your nonprofit should contribute to building a legacy. If not, you are preparing for the death of what you are striving to build. People will forget about your organization and mission work in the years to come.

What Makes an Effective Nonprofit?

To a significant extent, a nonprofit's effectiveness depends on your goals as a donor. For you, effectiveness will mean delivering results on issues you deem important. That being said, we are going to address five qualities and characteristics that are common in effective nonprofits. Organizations with these elements are likely to deliver results and have an impact. Keep in mind: Effective nonprofits—and those having the potential to be effective—are often underfinanced and stretched to their limits. Many worthy nonprofits suffer cash flow problems, poorly developed finance, management, and fundraising systems, and inadequate staff and board training. If you are open to strengthening those organizations aligned with your goals, then huge opportunities emerge for you as a donor.

Qualities and Characteristics Common to Effective Nonprofits

Clear mission and purpose. The most fundamental quality of an effective nonprofit is clarity about its mission—both what it seeks to accomplish and why this purpose is important. The nonprofit should communicate its mission clearly to all its stakeholders—board, staff, donors, volunteers, partners, and the general public—so that everyone understands its goals and works toward a common purpose. All the nonprofit's programs and operations should be aligned to advance its mission.

Ability to perform key functions. Effective nonprofits are able to perform essential functions necessary to fulfill their missions. The authors of *How Effective Nonprofits Work* cite six essential functions:

- Communicate vision and mission.
- Engage and seek stakeholders' input in designing programs, include people who use its services, and serve its target community appropriately.
- Achieve results and track impact against a few key measures, at least through basic means.
- Manage an active and informed governance structure.
- Secure resources appropriate to its needs.
- Plan for the future.

Strong practices, procedures, and policies. Effective nonprofits also follow good practices in three functional areas: finance, governance, and organizational/program development (thanks to *How Effective Nonprofits Work* for this framework). Donors expect the following:

- Annual audit delivered upon request
- Solid financial management processes

- Strong leadership team
- Evaluations of offered programs
- A strategic plan
- Committed staff members
- Positive feedback from people you serve

Good people. Above all, nonprofits depend on qualified, skilled, and talented board members, staff, and volunteers to fulfill their missions. Boards should be diverse, talent-rich, informed, and responsible about stewardship, dedicated to the nonprofit and not their self-interest, and above all, engaged. When nonprofits lack the resources and know-how to recruit and train effective board members, their governance, oversight, and leadership suffer accordingly.

Ability to mobilize others. The ability to mobilize and engage volunteers, other nonprofits, businesses, and government agencies is an essential skill for nonprofits seeking to address the root causes of problems and bring about long-term change. Building awareness and support among key audiences and bringing more people and resources to the table are essential to change. If change is one of your goals, look for nonprofits that have the following characteristics or develop them in your favorite organizations:

Clarifying Your Values and Goals for Philanthropy

Identifying the impact that you want to make will help you narrow the field of potential grantees to those that fit your values, goals, and interests. Clarifying your goals also opens up opportunities to build and strengthen those groups aligned with your interests, helping them accomplish the work you care about. What kinds of nonprofits do you most want to support, build, and strengthen? Here are some questions to help you clarify the values and goals for your philanthropy:

- What are your values?
- What do you want to achieve with your giving, volunteering, and even your skills and experience?
- What difference do you want to see in your community or society?
- At what level do you wish to make change?

<u>Scanning the Field for Potential Grantees</u>

Good ways to scan the field for grantees include talking with local foundations, organizations, and individuals who are knowledgeable in your areas of interest. These may include university researchers, business leaders, government agencies, associations, journalists, and other donors and foundations. Make a list of potential grantees, and add and update it as you scan. Through your conversations, you will identify organizations that are particularly effective or have good potential. Keep in mind the level at which you wish to make change, so that you can consider and compare organizations that do similar work. For example, if you wish to support groups that advocate for greater access to quality early education, then you will want to focus on organizations that make advocacy part of their mission. Your scan may also reveal useful information about which strategies are successful for accomplishing the work you care about.

How do you start a nonprofit organization?

Step 1: Do Your Homework

Conduct a needs analysis. Find out if organizations (nonprofit, for-profit, or government) are already doing the same or similar work in your community. It will be harder to get support if you are just duplicating existing services, versus improving or adding to them. Also find demographic or population data that shows a need for your services, and explain how that need is not being met.

Is a nonprofit right for you? Public charities must be <u>organized</u> and <u>operated</u> exclusively for <u>exempt purposes</u> set forth in section 501(c)(3) of the Internal Revenue Code. If you want to start a nonprofit so you can get grants to pay yourself a salary, stop now and find another option. Realistically, many new nonprofits aren't even ready or eligible to get grants.

Know the alternatives. Forming a new nonprofit might be the most complicated way to act on your passion to serve your community. The biggest challenge for most new nonprofits is to develop and maintain reliable income streams. Estimates vary, but most experts agree that less than half of nonprofit startups survive beyond five years. Of those that survive, perhaps one-third are in financial distress.

Step 2: Build a Solid Foundation

Draft your mission statement. Developing your mission statement is a critical first step. It communicates your nonprofit's purpose, what groups it serves, and how it will serve them. Every decision and action in your organization should support and further your mission.

Write a business plan. Just as with a for-profit business, a business plan can help a nonprofit describe how it intends to achieve its mission in more specific details. It also can be used to outline a new project or venture.

Develop your board. As your nonprofit's governing body, your board fulfills a variety of roles and <u>legal responsibilities</u>. In order to carry out these duties effectively, the board will change as your organization grows and matures. While <u>recruitment</u> is an important step in this process, a systematic approach to <u>board development</u>, including orientation, training, evaluation, and the cultivation of prospective board members, is critical to ensuring its long-term success.

Step 3: Incorporate Your Nonprofit

Why should you incorporate?
- Having a formal structure will give credibility to your programs and services.
- The corporate structure limits the liability of the organization's officers and directors.
- The IRS requires organizing documents and governance policies and procedures that are usually associated with corporations.

Step 4: File for 501(c)(3) Tax-Exempt Status

<u>Apply for exempt status with the Internal Revenue Service (IRS)</u>. Be aware, there is a user fee, depending on whether you expect your average annual gross receipts to exceed $10,000 annually over a four-year period. It also can take 3-12 months for the IRS to return its decision, depending on how many questions the IRS has about your application.

Step 5: Ongoing Compliance

Register with your state's agency that regulates charitable organizations and charitable solicitations (usually the Attorney General). Again, registration requirements will vary with each state.

Prepare for annual reporting requirements. All exempt orgs must file some version of <u>Form 990</u> with the IRS. Which version you file will depend on your total gross receipts for the year. Form 990 shows your finances, activities, governance processes, directors, and key staff, which are open to public inspection. States have their own reporting and renewal requirements, too, and these can vary with each state. Thus, consider tracking your org's finances and activities in such a way that will help these annual reporting requirements to be met smoothly.

Journal Entry

Do you want to start a nonprofit? If so, why?

What is your charitable mission work?

What are your goals after reading this chapter?

1.

2.

3.

CHAPTER FIVE
DON'T CHOOSE FAILURE

Starting a new business or turning your side hustle into your main hustle is very exciting. You caught the vision and now it is time to stay the course until you see something spectacular. Sadly, many business ventures fail for various reasons. Failure is an option, but don't make that your choice. For example, take the real estate industry. In 2007, this industry took a turn for the worse and those who were invested suffered a great loss and are still losing. Therefore, failure does exist if you were considering starting a real estate company. However, a good business model and strategy can absorb downturns. I recall hearing a story of a young lady who had all of her assets tied up in real estate. Per her explanation, failure was inevitable because her investment pool only consisted of real estate. In cases like this, you lose. If banks loaned you money, they lose. If you are a nonprofit, funders/donors lose.

At one point, it was reported that 40% of all organizations go under within the first year and 65% within the first five years. Even now, the Small Business Administration (SBA) reports that half of all employer establishments survive at least five years and a third survive 10 years. This is a far cry from what was previously reported, but it is good news for you, the new business owner. This chapter is written to help you understand why failures exist so you will be less likely to fall victim to them. To follow are the top 7 reasons new businesses fail and some basic tips for avoiding them.

The first reason businesses fail is **they start for the wrong reason**. You should not start a business because you want to make a lot of money. Or have more time with your family. Or so you do not have to answer to anyone else. You should start because you have a passion and great love for what you do. Start for the mental stamina it will bring and the challenges it will help you overcome. If you started your business for any of these reasons, you have a good chance of becoming successful in the business that you started. These characteristics will fuel your drive to keep going when others want you to throw in the towel. Through the process, you learn that failure is an option, but for you, failure transitions into learning opportunities.

Secondly, new businesses fail due to **poor management**. There are many research findings that cite poor management as one of the top reasons businesses fail. New businesses owners know how to do the work, perform the day-to-day tasks, and even engage with customers. However, many lack relevant business management experience. Experience in managing business finances, purchasing, and hiring are where I see the largest gaps. New business owners are forced to muddle through these tasks on their own because they cannot afford to hire professionals to help them. When the business owner works in the business, it is difficult for them to hire and train helpers. They tend to want the individual(s) to do everything the way they would. I can't tell you how unrealistic this is. A good manager must learn to trust others to carry the reigns.

Lacking the capital to start the business is also one of the most common reasons for failure. One of the most fatal mistakes made is not estimating the amount of money needed to start your business and keep you afloat for at least one year while the business is built. This an increase from ten years ago, when the recommendation was to have six months of reserves. The reserves should include business and personal estimates. Keep in mind that a business usually takes more than a year to really get going and three to five years to reap a profit.

This may not apply to everyone, because most businesses start out of a home, but starting a brick and motor **location** is another reason why new businesses do not succeed. A good location will help a struggling business to strive. Things that you want to consider are customer accessibility, parking, location of competitors, conditions and safety of the building, the availability of incentive programs in that area for start-up businesses, and the type of businesses that have been in that location before. A good location can provoke turn around for a failing business and cause them to strive. A bad location could be disastrous even if you offer a good service or product.

One of my personal favorites is that businesses fail because of a **failure to plan**. You've probably heard the saying, "if you fail to plan, you plan to fail." It's simple, but it's true and it's very profound. So is the contrary. Any person who has carried out a successful major event had to engage in methodical strategic planning.

At one point, it was reported that 40% of all organizations go under within the first year and 65% within the first five years.

The same can be said for most businesses that succeed. It is critical that you not only have a business plan, but that you also have a strategic plan. Many businesses fail because of fundamental and foundational elements that really were in the owner's control. Often, crisis could have been averted if there had been a plan in place. In addition, most bankers will require a business plan, marketing plan, and maybe even a strategic plan.

Your business plan can be written in such a way that it will serve as your strategic plan for the next one to three years.

To accomplish this, include all of the sections discussed in the first chapter of this book, but also go the extra mile to include a SWOT Analysis (see Chapter 6) and organizational goals. For those of you who have already started your business, it's never too late to go back and complete this foundational work.

Expanding too early is a leading cause of business failure. As business owners, we sometimes confuse success with the need to expand our business. I recall assisting an organization with a plan to roll out one program per year. They decided instead to roll out 7 programs in one year without perfecting any of them. In their case, they chose quantity over quality. As a result, none of their programs were sustainable. The number is never more important than the quality. It is best to perfect a few things than to offer imperfection in a lot of things. Besides, all growth is not good growth. Sometimes, growth is infection.

Start with one service or product and perfect it before adding others. Make sure your first location is running like a well-oiled machine before opening another one. What happens if you transfer the dysfunction of one product or service to another or from one location to another? When you expand too soon, the dysfunction is spread out and harder to contain. Not to evoke fear in you, but the result of expanding too soon is closing your doors. Before expanding, always consider the resources that you will need. Decide how many additional people you will need, what the details will be of the additional location, and what your customer base will be in the expansion. In short, decide what you need to make your business grow. With the right systems and people in place, you can focus on business growth and not on doing everything yourself.

In the age of technology and social media, **not having an internet presence** can definitely cause your business to fail. If you have a business, you need a website and social media accounts.

According to the US Department of Commerce, in the United States alone, 77% of the population use the internet and 65 billion people make online purchases. The numbers continue to rise every year. You need to be present and accounted for. At the very least, every business should have a professional-looking website/page. This makes it easy for consumers to find your business and secure your services and products. Without an internet presence, you are leaving money on the table and losing business to your competitors who do have a website and social media interaction. Personally, I always look at a company's website before I do business with them. That's not to say I bypass them if they don't have a website, but it helps a great deal with information seeking.

Lastly, when it comes to understanding failure, realize that **you are the face of your business** and ultimately the secret to your success. As much as I try to avoid it, when people greet me, they call me "sunshine" or "that sunshine lady." What would happen if I was sloppy in my dealings? I don't believe any of us enter into business planning to fail. Some are born into a business, however, most of the entrepreneurs who have achieved great success started with nothing and from scratch. They had something that set them apart personally and professionally. For example, Bill Gates and Steve Jobs had an openness to new knowledge and a willingness to learn that I believe set them apart and positioned them for success. What sets you apart?

There are six strategies that I recommend for new and existing business owners to thrive. If you can recall, in December 2007, the economy took a nosedive. The recession impacted everyone. It didn't matter if you were or weren't the owner of a business or home. One of the reasons for the nosedive was the mortgage industry. At the time, people were allowed to borrow money that they could not afford to pay back. They were approved for loans even when they weren't creditworthy. They were given money for houses that exceeded the appraised value. During that time, it seemed like the economy was booming, but eventually the market reached a saturation point and began to crash.

Can you imagine the impact on those who were in the real estate business? People who once held over a million dollars in revenue probably found themselves barely netting $100,000. The level of the business and the lifestyle of the business owner was created around a booming market. What happens when the market is not booming anymore? The following strategies will help you to lay the proper foundation from the beginning and stay on track when economic issues arise.

Starting a business can be tough, but growing the business is even harder. Don't ever lose sight of why you went into business. Keep that reason at the forefront of your mind. In doing so, the passion you have will be ignited and allow you to have periodic reality checks. If I could give one piece of advice about passion, it would be to always stay open to readjusting and going back to the drawing board. There are many ways to get things done and be successful.

You must take time away from your business so that you can work on your business. You should do this at least on a weekly basis. If nothing else, take two hours each week to research trends in your industry, work on your growth plan, build your customer base, or meet with a mentor. Plan to go to retreats and conferences that relate to your industry. You have to seek ways to refresh yourself while enhancing and strengthening your organization.

Continue to work on your marketing. It doesn't matter how long you have been in business. Don't be afraid to invest money in marketing. Keeping your business in the view of consumers is a huge precursor to growth. Typically, marketing dollars don't make the budget or they are the first to get cut. But the reality is, as a new and/or existing business, you can't afford not to market. View marketing as paying yourself. No marketing, no customers. No customers, no sales. No sales, no revenue. No revenue, no business. Don't spend money in your business until you determine your monthly marketing budget.

Increase your email marketing. It doesn't have to be anything grand. You can simply place a spot on your website where people can sign up for your mailing list. You can use the list to send email blasts. This is a very inexpensive way to keep your business in front of consumers. There are many free resources you can use to help with email marketing. Social media is also a way to reach new and existing customers.

Gather a motivated team, even if it is made up of volunteers, friends or family members. You should not have to work hard convincing the team to buy into the vision. If you have to work too hard to get a person to see the vision, then maybe they should be a supporter from a distance. You will interact with everyone, but you don't have to place them on your team.

New customers are great, but use the bulk of your resources to keep your existing customers. You have to continue to develop and nurture previously established relationships. Customers who trust the integrity of your business want to and will buy more from you. There are businesses that I frequent because they value their customers. In many cases, their prices are not the cheapest, but I spend with them because I can see the investment they make in their customers. Rewarding existing customers who purchase more is cheaper than acquiring new customers.

New and existing business owners are creating their own destinies and paving their own paths. It's all about individuals and teams using their passions and dreams to create enterprises. These enterprises will sustain families and contribute to local and national economies. The excitement I had when I started my business years ago is the same excitement that I have today, thousands of clients later. It is time for you to thrive!

Journal Entry

What enlightened you most in this chapter?

Why do you refuse to fail? Draft a success statement/creed.

What are your goals after reading this chapter?

1.

2.

3.

CHAPTER SIX
PLAN TO SUCCEED

You are not thinking more than one year ahead when starting a business. Your motivation may simply be keeping a roof over your head and food on the table. When you are missing opportunities because you are unfocused or have gotten off the path, it is time to strategically plan. Strategic planning is an important part of the creation, development, and growth of any organization. New organizations that are interested in growth are not exempt from planning. Planning helps the organization map out strategic steps to achieve its goals. Organizations can experience a level of success without a plan, but those who invest time and resources to develop a specific strategy can achieve success at a much quicker pace.

Strategic planning is an organization's process of defining its strategy or direction and making decisions on allocating its resources to pursue this strategy, including its capital or people. While most business owners shudder at the idea of creating or revising strategic plans, they are instrumental in strengthening and growing your business. The beauty of having a written plan is that once all of the time and effort is invested in the plan, it is just a matter of overseeing the plan to completion. A SWOT analysis is a great exercise to go through because it identifies the key areas of the organization that may need targeted resources, pointing out opportunities and opposing issues. The SWOT analysis process can flush out many great ideas to help target development, growth, and improvement.

To begin the SWOT process, think about the following:
- Strengths: Characteristics of the organization that may give it an advantage over others;
- Weaknesses: Characteristics of the organization that may be a disadvantage as related to others;
- Opportunities: Conditions outside the organization that could potentially increase funding or revenue;
- Threats: Conditions outside the organization that could create problems for the organization.

By following these seven simple steps given by Robert Stover, you'll find that creating a strategic plan is simpler and quicker than you ever thought it would be.

Step One: Where Are You Now?

In this step, we take a look at the two major drivers of strategic planning: stuff that is happening now or stuff we think is about to happen to our business.

That can be good stuff, but it's usually bad stuff.

So, in step one, we get clear on the problems, challenges, and future dangers facing your business. Then we narrow them down to those that will create the most impact.

Step Two: What's The Vision?

While problems and challenges drive the need for strategic thinking, it is vision that drives the rest of the strategy process.

Nothing happens until you have a vision. The clearer and more compelling your vision is, the more powerful and imaginative your strategy will be.

The vision you craft in this step will act as the "North Star" to the rest of your strategic planning process.

Your vision should include tangible targets like revenue goals, market share goals, etc., as well as intangibles like values, culture, and purpose.

Step Three: What Are the Obstacles?

To have a vision is to have obstacles. They appear the minute your vision is formed.

Yet, many business leaders have trouble taking a realist's perspective and looking big obstacles squarely in the eye.

Recognizing major obstacles to your vision does not make you a pessimist. The purpose of looking at obstacles is not to look for excuses and reasons not to pursue the vision. It's to look at what our strategy must overcome, so that it can be as effective as possible.

Failure to look at obstacles and adapt your strategy to them creates nasty surprises.

Looking at big, scary obstacles realistically gives the imagination the fuel it needs to craft innovative strategies for victory.

Step Four: What are our resources?

Only after you know what the dangers are, what your vision for the future is, and what's standing in the way, are you ready to look at your resources.

We are looking for two major elements: what resources we have to help us achieve our vision and what resources we need.

Why not do this first—before the vision? Won't a vision be more realistic if we first look to resources?

The truth is, a resource often isn't a resource until a vision gives it meaning and use.

A rock at my campsite isn't a resource until I discover that I forgot a hammer to pound on the tent stakes—or a bear is threatening my life.

In the same way, you've got "rocks" lying around your business that you would never think to use until a compelling vision gives them meaning as a resource.

Step Five: What's our strategy?

Strategy exists to serve a vision.

Vision and resources answer the questions, "Where do we want to go?" and "Where are we now?" Strategy answers the question, "How do we get there?"

During this step, you'll take a look at your resources, mix in some imagination, and create a path around, under, or over your obstacles to take you to your vision in the fastest way possible.

Step Six: What are our tactics?

Now that we know our major strategic direction, it's time to get specific with details, timetables, and accountabilities.

Tactics answer the question, "Who's going to do what by when?"

Ironically, if you, or a member of your team, excels at vision and imagination, this will be the toughest step.

On the other hand, if you are a realist and know all that "dreaming" won't make anything happen, this will be your favorite step. Either way, nothing will happen until you complete this step in the strategic thinking process.

It's time to make something happen!

Step Seven: What will we monitor and measure?

In the late 1800's, famed military strategist Field Marshall Helmuth Carl Bernard von Moltke noted, "No battle plan survives contact with the enemy."

What's interesting is that this quote was from a military man who was known to take thousands of variables into account when crafting his battle plan.

His point being: Things change. You better adapt to them.

Vision is about the future, and strategy is how to get there. Yet, no person knows the future—nor will any amount of intense data gathering fully reveal the future.

Therefore, we need to constantly monitor our strategy and tactics, making adjustments where necessary to keep us driving towards our vision.

Too often, I see business leaders get so locked on a specific strategy or tactic that they fail to realize when it is time to try something different.

Monitoring and measuring the right things is the only way to keep you on track and on time.

It's Your Future...

Neither you nor I can predict what will happen in the future. But we've been given the amazing ability to shape it in ways no one else can imagine.

This simple, seven-step process will help you move from today's challenges and frustrations to a richer future.
SMARTER Goals

Goals can be powerful motivators for individuals and organizations, if done right. If done poorly, however, they can have an *opposite* effect, i.e., *lowering* motivation and desire for improvement. To be done right, goals must be SMARTER (**S**pecific, **M**easurable, **A**greed, **R**ealistic, Time-Bound, **E**thical, and **R**ecorded).

1. Specific
Exactly what is it you want to achieve in your organization? A good goal statement explains the what, why, who, where, and when of a goal. If your goal statement is vague, you will find it hard to achieve because it will be difficult to define success.

2. Measurable
You must be able to track progress and measure the result of your goal. A good goal statement describes how much or how many. How will I know when I have achieved my goal?

3. Agreed
Your goal must be relevant to your stakeholders and agreed on. Examples of people needed to agree with your goal are your line manager, employees, and customers.

4. Realistic
Your goal should be stretching but realistic and relevant to you and your organization. Make sure the actions you need to take to

achieve your goal are within your control. Is your goal achievable?

5. Time-Bound
Goals must have a deadline. A good goal statement will project when you will achieve your goal. Without time limits, it's easy to put goals off and leave them to die. Along with a deadline, it's a good idea to set some short-term milestones along the way to help you measure progress.

6. Ethical
Goals must sit comfortably within your moral compass. Most people resist acting unethically. Set goals that meet a high ethical standard.

7. Recorded
Always write down your goal before you start working toward it. Written goals are visible and have a greater chance of success. The recording is necessary for the planning, monitoring, and reviewing of progress. Is your goal written down?

SMARTER Goal Action Plan Template

Goal:	
Outcome/Results	

Action & Timeline	Action Steps	Time-line

Support Network	
Obstacles	
Adjustments	

SMARTER Goal Action Plan Template

Goal:	
Outcome/Results	

Action & Timeline	Action Steps	Timeline
Support Network		
Obstacles		
Adjustments		

SMARTER Goal Action Plan Template

Goal:	
Outcome/Results	

Action & Timeline	Action Steps	Time-line

Support Network	
Obstacles	
Adjustments	

Journal Entry

How can you use the information in this chapter?

What are your goals after reading this chapter?

1.

2.

3.

CHAPTER SEVEN
BUSINESS BRANDING

Brand building is simply a new label for a collection of functions that have *always* been necessary to make a business successful, requiring ongoing effort in several areas to:

- Increase the public's awareness of your business name and logo.
- Build a strong company "essence" that inspires loyalty and trust in your current customers and provides a level of familiarity and comfort to draw in potential customers.

Often referred to as the "good will" portion of your business, your brand is intangible and has nothing at all to do with any real estate, inventory, or vehicle fleets your company may count as assets. Instead, it refers to the reputation behind your company's name and logo. A carefully built brand is worth more in actual dollars than all the tangible assets put together and is what will reap monetary rewards when you're ready to sell your company. The first thing you have to do is decide how you want people to perceive your business, and then figure out what you have to do to get there.

So what goes into building your brand? Here's a look:

Consistency in advertising: Decide what you can do for your customers that your competitors can't and hammer away at those points in every ad. Create a "sell line" that defines your company in a nutshell and use it.

Customer service: Only employ people who can get on board with your brand, and make sure that each person understands his or her part in building it. Once a customer is ignored at the counter or treated poorly on the phone or on the sales floor, you've lost not only that person but everyone else that hears about the unfortunate experience. Remember that word-of-mouth can help, but it can also hurt. Get rid of employees who won't cooperate, even if they're related to you!

Public relations: Keep promises you make. See that your customers aren't disappointed with what they find once your advertising gets them through the door. Make it easy for them to make purchases and returns. They should leave smiling. If you tell your local Little League team that you'll provide team T-shirts, follow through. If you commit to a joint venture with another business, school, or group of any kind, keep up your end of the deal. Pay your invoices on time. Be a good citizen. Get involved with community projects where your business can do something positive (and maybe get some free press).

Your willingness to use the internet: A company with no web presence is archaic. Even if you're only interested in local sales right now, your customers are on the web, and they'll want to see you there, too. Get it done now.

Below I've gathered the top five tips you can use right now to make your small business brand distinct.

1. Know Your Audience
Marketing has evolved into a pull economy and brands must be more than a logo or a design. They have to build meaningful relationships with their customers. To do this, you must know your audience, their needs and desires, and their struggles and challenges to progress. You must understand how and why they purchase, and the channels they use to interact with businesses like yours.

Within your wider audience is your niche—those prospects who benefit the most from the services you offer. Tailor your brand and your marketing primarily to this niche rather than trying to appeal to everyone at once. As you expand into new markets, you will add niches and craft targeted marketing for each. When you market with niches, you can design value propositions with each target market in mind, addressing their distinct needs and triggers.

2. Know Yourself

Just how do you craft a brand that compels your audience? The answer to that lies in discovering and articulating your brand values—that is, the passion and purpose behind your company. What inspired you to create the business? What value do you offer your customers?

Avoid superficial values or vague statements about profit and revenue. Your brand values should be earnest and enthusiastic declarations that reflect the winning qualities of a memorable brand. You might hold authenticity above all else, or strive to be the simplest solution to a common problem. Whatever business you're in, you have something vital to offer your prospects. Focus on that as your reason for being and customers will take notice.
While some brands find their identity in fighting against something, avoid comparisons to the competition. Keep the conversation positive and focus on your brand values and your product's benefits, not what the competition doesn't do.

3. Communicate Effectively

First impressions set the standard for every future interaction. Start with authority and clarity and follow through with responsibility and superb customer service. How effectively you communicate about your product can have more impact on your success than the product itself. Even when a customer has a negative experience, with open and honest communication, you have the opportunity to turn that person into a brand evangelist.

Treat all stakeholders with honesty and respect and the word will spread that you're a company to be trusted. Brands who invest time and energy in effective communication foster long term relationships with customers and generate immeasurable goodwill.

4. Design to Impress
Compelling brands are instantly recognizable. They have a style and design that is unique, evokes emotion, and is relevant to their niche market. Quality graphic design should be a part of every one of your marketing materials. Your website, logo, brochures, and emails should all be designed for maximum aesthetic appeal. Beauty and elegance exude professionalism and trigger feelings of comfort and reassurance, which reinforces the value of your brand in the customer's mind.

Impressive design doesn't always mean graphics and animation. Typography, page layout, UX design, and design for readability are all important factors in an engaging and effective brand image. What's most important is to design to impress your niche.

5. Be Consistent
Chances are, you know what a Pepsi tastes like. You can visualize an iPod, taste a Twinkie, and recall the smell of your partner's favorite perfume or cologne.

One of the inherent values of a small business brand is that it's familiar. Without consistency, businesses never have the opportunity to evolve into sustainable brands. Consistency builds trust, breeds recognition, and in the long-term, drives greater profits. Capitalize on your brand values, your impressive design, and your intimate understanding of your audience by delivering a consistently enjoyable brand experience. You will become known for more than just a product or service, but for invoking a particular feeling in your customers.

Every communication about your brand should articulate what is best and most compelling about you. By uniting research, design, and message consistency, you can develop long-lasting and profitable relationships with your ideal prospects. Early branding of a small or emerging company is key to business success. It is the quickest way for your company to express what it is and what it can offer. Inaccurate branding of a new business can make it difficult for people to grasp why the business exists in the first place.

Journal Entry

What are your initial thoughts about branding your organization?

What are your top 3 priorities?

What are your goals after reading this chapter?

1.

2.

3.

Notes:

Thank you for your support. I pray this book was a blessing to you. To order additional copies of this book, to invite Alisa to speak at your event, or to bring a workshop to your ministry, contact her at:

Alisa J. Henley
PO Box 683
Grandview, MO 64030
1 888 851 5554

info@alisahenley.com   www.alisahenley.com

For ministry consulting services, visit www.u-shine.org.

Other published books:

Catch The Vision, Stay the Course!
ISBN: 978-0-9646543-5-8

Chronicles, Covered & Revealed
ISBN: 978-0692-2751-8-4

GEMS, Fruit of the Spirit
ISBN-13: 978-0692-4402-5-4

www.ingramcontent.com/pod-product-compliance
Lightning Source LLC
Chambersburg PA
CBHW060405190526
45169CB00002B/756